Wild UNDERGROUND

Caves and Caving

NEIL CHAMPION

Smart Apple Media

Published by Smart Apple Media, an imprint of Black Rabbit Books
P.O. Box 3263, Mankato, Minnesota 56002
www.blackrabbitbooks.com

Printed in the United States of America at Corporate Graphics,
North Mankato, Minnesota

Library of Congress Cataloging-in-Publication Data
Champion, Neil.
 Wild underground : caves and caving / by Neil Champion.
     p. cm. -- (Adventure outdoors)
 Includes index.
 Summary: "Explores underground caves and the sport of caving
by discussing cave formations, the gear and equipment needed,
and the five different cave grades. Introduces famous caves
around the world and includes picture labels and a reading
quiz"--Provided by publisher.
 ISBN 978-1-59920-810-7 (library binding)
1. Caving--Juvenile literature. I. Title.
 GV200.62.C43 2013
 796.52'5--dc23
                                2012002526

Created by Appleseed Editions Ltd,
Designed and illustrated by Guy Callaby
Edited by Mary-Jane Wilkins
Picture research by Su Alexander

PO1443
2-2012

9 8 7 6 5 4 3 2 1

Contents

Let's Go Caving! 4

How Are Caves Formed? 6

Inside Caves 8

Getting Started 10

Technical Caving Gear 12

Thinking about Safety 14

Knots for Cavers 16

Going Underground 18

Squeezes and Siphons 20

Amazing Rock Formations 22

Extreme Caving 24

Caving Around the World 26

What do you know about caving? 28

Glossary 30

Websites and Books 31

Index 32

Let's Go Caving!

People go caving all over the world. There are large caves that extend for many miles in the United States, Mexico, China, France, Britain, Italy, Slovenia, Australia, and New Zealand—to name just a few countries.

Caving is an exciting activity, which takes you to beautiful and mysterious places underground. It can be dangerous, so you need to learn how to do it safely with experienced people.

A caver explores a huge cavern by flashlight.

Amazing FACTS

Ancient peoples painted on the walls and ceilings of caves. Most of their paintings have been found in Europe. About 350 caves in France and Spain contain **prehistoric** paintings. The paintings show important aspects of their lives, such as hunting scenes. Some paintings also contain handprints. Two famous caves in France, called Lascaux and Chauvet, have superb and well-preserved paintings. The paintings in Chauvet were discovered in 1994 and have been dated using a technique called radiocarbon dating, which shows that they are about 32,000 years old.

This prehistoric animal painting was found on the wall of a cave.

Taking Up the Challenge

For thousands of years, people used caves as homes, religious spaces, and places in which to store or hide things. Geologists and archaeologists have explored them for hundreds of years to find out about the earth and what is under our feet. Caving as a sport started about 120 years ago when enthusiasts first experienced the thrill of going underground where no one had been before.

TRUE Survivors

One early caving **pioneer** was a Frenchman called Edouard-Alfred Martel (1859–1938). He explored caves in France as well as in Britain, the United States, Greece, Turkey, Montenegro, Norway, and Spain. Martel was a born survivor, often having to escape from landslides and underground flooding. He used ropes to get in and out of many caves and developed early techniques for doing this.

How Are Caves Formed?

Caves are formed naturally on coastlines by waves crashing against cliffs or inland when rainwater and underground rivers react with a type of rock called **limestone**.

The water creates vast networks of hollows and tunnels in the rock. In volcanic areas, **lava** can make caves, and some **glaciers** around the world contain ice caves.

A coastal cave formed as the result of the constant battering of the cliffs by waves

Amazing FACTS

The largest cave in the world is in Vietnam. It is called the Son Doong Cave and was found by local people in 1991. One chamber is over 3 miles (5 km) long, 853 feet (260 m) high, and 492 feet (150 m) wide. A small jungle grows in part of the cave.

Artificial lighting in a show cave highlights the walls and ceilings of this underground world.

Show Caves

Tourist caves have been made safe for people who have no caving experience to visit and see the wonders of the world underground. Visitors usually have to pay a fee to enter and are given a guided tour. To make the caves safe, the floor is often flattened or covered and lighting is installed. The oldest known tourist cave is the Postojna Cave in Slovenia. Records show that there were guided tours there in 1213, almost 800 years ago! Real cavers prefer wild caves.

Wild Caves

Wild caves have no man-made safety features, such as artificial floors or lighting. Only experienced cavers should go into wild caves. Groups venturing into wild caves need to take their own lighting, ropes, ladders, and other special equipment to deal with whatever they encounter. They also need caving knowledge and experience.

TRUE Survivors

Evidence has been found in a cave on the island of Jersey in the English Channel which shows that **Neanderthal** people lived on the site for a quarter of a million years and died out only about 30,000 years ago. They left evidence in the form of many thousands of tools, which were mostly made from stone.

Inside Caves

There are caves in most countries around the world. They range from small hollows in cliffs and hills to enormous, complex tunnels and passages that run for many miles underground.

The stalagmites and stalactites in this limestone cave were formed over millions of years.

Limestone Caves

Caves in limestone areas can be deep and long, with many large chambers and narrow passages. There may be places where you have to climb and others where you **abseil**. Interesting caves are perfect for exploring. They are still being discovered around the world, and known caves are constantly being extended when people find new passages that link different cave systems.

Limestone caves are formed by water flowing underground and carving out tunnels and chambers. Water dripping from the ceilings can form amazing structures, such as towering stalagmites and hanging stalactites. These build up over time when the limestone rock is dissolved in water and then reforms when it is **deposited**. Sheet-like deposits of calcite called flowstone are another feature of limestone caves. Some caves are dry, while others contain rivers and even lakes. Some are cold and some are warm, depending on where in the world they are.

10 Ceki 2, Slovenia, 4,927 ft. (1,502 m)

9 Sima de la Cornisa, Spain, 4,944 ft. (1,507 m)

8 Shakta Vjacheslav Pantjukhina, Georgia, 4,948 ft. (1,508 m)

7 Sarma, Georgia, 5,062 ft. (1,543 m)

6 Torca del Cerro del Cuevon, Spain, 5,213 ft. (1,589 m)

5 Réseau Jean Bernard, France, 5,256 ft. (1,602 m)

4 Vogelschact and Lamprechtsofen, Austria, 5,354 ft. (1,632 m)

3 Gouffre Mirolda, France, 5,686 ft. (1,733 m)

2 Illuzia-Snezhnaja-Mezhonnogo, Georgia, 5,755 ft. (1,754 m)

1 Krubera-Voronja Cave, Georgia, 7,188 ft. (2,191 m)

Amazing FACTS

The longest cave system in the world is in Kentucky. The Mammoth Cave is an incredible 390 miles (628 km) long and part of Mammoth Cave **National Park**. That makes it more than twice as long as its nearest rival, Jewel Cave in South Dakota. The cave has about 150 miles (241 km) of passages.

Getting Started

For cavers, danger is mixed with the thrill of going where few other people have been before. You need to learn skills, such as how to abseil and ascend a rope, and gain experience underground so you can match yourself safely against the challenges of caving.

Join a Club

Many countries have caving clubs with junior sections. Joining one of these is the best way to learn how to go safely into a cave system. Start by going with experienced adults into straightforward caves where you do not need special skills, moving on to more challenging places where you might need to abseil or climb.

These young cavers in Canada are having fun and getting dirty underground!

Crawling through narrow gaps is tough on your clothing.

What to Wear

Find out if the cave you plan to visit will be cold or warm or wet or dry and choose your clothes accordingly. Caves are dirty places, so wear tough, old clothing.

For exploring cold caves, wear **base layer thermals** under warm pants and a sweatshirt or warm fleece. In a wet cave, you will need a waterproof outer layer. You may even need a wetsuit if there are underground rivers.

If the cave is warm, cotton clothes are fine. Wear tennis shoes or walking boots, depending on conditions. You may also need leather gloves, **neoprene** socks, and even knee and elbow pads if you have to crawl far.

TRUE Survivors

The Lechuguilla Cave is in the Carlsbad Caverns National Park, New Mexico. It is the sixth longest cave system in the world at 130 miles (210 km) and the deepest in the US at 1,604 feet (489 m). In 1991, Emily Mobley was part of a team of cavers who planned to spend several days exploring underground. However, their plans had to change when a boulder fell on Mobley, shattering her leg. The team had a doctor with them, but they were a long way from safety. More than 20 rescuers took four days to bring Mobley safely out of the cave system, setting up pulleys and carrying her stretcher on their backs through tight passages.

If the cave is dry and easy to walk through, you can wear lighter clothing.

Technical Caving Gear

You need special equipment when you are going deep underground into a dark, cold, and wet place. A helmet, headlamp, ropes, ladders, harness, and special climbing devices are all useful. Make sure you get expert training— from how to put a helmet and harness on to how to abseil safely.

A young caver wearing a helmet and headlamp

headlamp

caving helmet

Lighting the Dark

A flashlight (plus a spare as a backup) is important. Most cavers use a headlamp which can be worn around a helmet and stays in place. A headlamp always faces the way you are facing, and wearing one leaves your hands free to do other things. Powerful **halogen** lamps send out a great beam but use battery energy fast. **LED** lights are more efficient. You can also use a carbide lamp, which uses a chemical reaction rather than batteries to provide light.

Going Down and Coming Up

There are several devices that can help you when going up or down a rope. When you are abseiling, you have to trust the rope, harness, and a device that acts as a brake as you descend. Make sure an expert prepares you and your equipment and that someone is standing below when you go down.

Climbing a rope takes practice and will feel difficult at first. Again, you must learn with an expert who can watch you. For your first abseil and rope ascent, make sure you choose a short drop of about 32–50 feet (10–15 m).

A caver descends, or abseils, down a rope wearing a harness and using an abseil device.

TRUE Survivors

The Mexican splayfoot salamander is an amphibian that lives in crevices in humid caves in pine forests. It was first spotted in 1941 and had not been seen since so the **species** was thought to be **extinct**. In 2010, Sean Rovito, one of a team of scientists abseiling in large caves in Mexico, rediscovered this natural world survivor.

Thinking about Safety

Caves are dark and full of steep drops. Some are wet and cold enough to cause **hypothermia**. If you become lost, you may become physically exhausted as well as hungry and thirsty. Caves can also flood quickly if there is lots of rain above ground that may fill tunnels and passages.

Planning Prevents Problems

Good planning can prevent problems from happening in the first place, which is better than trying to cope once they arise.

HERE ARE SOME TOP PLANNING TIPS:

- Take plenty of warm and waterproof **CLOTHING** into cold and wet caves.

- Carry your extra gear in a **BACKPACK**.

- Take emergency **FOOD** and plenty of **WATER**.

- Take a **SPARE HEADLAMP** as a backup.

- **ONLY** go into a cave with people who have been there before and are experienced cavers. **NEVER GO ALONE**.

- Take a **MAP** and a description of the passages and chambers you will visit.

- Get an up-to-date **WEATHER FORECAST** to rule out the possibility of flooding.

- Make sure you have mastered essential skills such as **ASCENDING** and **DESCENDING** a rope.

Emergency Equipment

As well as a spare flashlight, take a first aid kit in case of accidents and learn some simple first aid techniques. Duct tape is useful for patching up torn clothing. A survival bag and pocket knife are two other useful items to take with you.

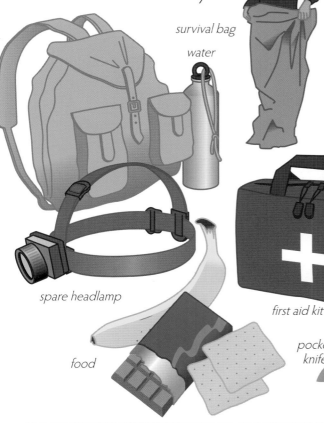

survival bag

water

spare headlamp

food

first aid kit

pocket knife

duct tape

Caves are full of hidden dangers, such as this fast-flowing river.

CAVING TRAGEDY

Occasionally a tragedy happens underground. In 1981, an experienced caver had an accident when he was exploring the Lost Creek Cave System in Colorado. Bruce Unger was deep underground and traversing a tricky part of a passage when his foot slipped on the wet surface and then became trapped in the fast-flowing water of an underground river. He lost his balance and drowned in the river. His body was not recovered until two weeks later.

Knots for Cavers

Knots are very useful to cavers and you need to know which knot you need in any situation. Here are a few of the most important knots you should know. Practice tying them over and over again, while watching TV or listening to music, so you can tie them perfectly.

Rethreaded Figure-Eight

This is the most common knot used to attach a rope to your harness.

1 Tie a figure-eight about 3 feet (1 m) from one end of the rope.

2 Thread the end of the rope to the attachment point of your harness (the manufacturer's notes tell you where this is on your harness).

harness

Have about 5 incles (12 cm) of tail left over.

3 Now rethread the figure-eight.

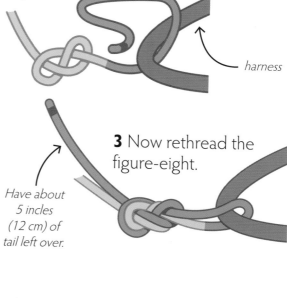

stopper knot

4 Finish with a stopper knot.

*Cavers use knots to attach ropes to a harness and to **anchors** in the rock.*

Figure-Eight on the Bight

You use this knot to attach a rope to an anchor or to your harness using a **carabiner**. It looks like the previous knot but is tied differently.

stopper knot

1 Take a **bight** (an open loop) of rope about 3 feet (1m) from the end and tie a figure-eight knot in the bight.

2 Finish off with a stopper knot.

Clove Hitch

Use this knot to attach yourself and your rope to an anchor. It will tighten if you put weight on to it and is very secure.

1 Make two loops in the rope as shown.

2 Put the second loop directly behind the first.

3 Attach the knot to a carabiner and tighten it.

Italian Hitch

This knot is also called a friction hitch and can be used to safeguard a caver climbing a difficult rock.

1 Make two loops in the rope like a clove hitch.

2 Your two loops will look like a pair of glasses. Break the glasses and bring the loops toward you.

3 Put a carabiner into the knot. You need one with a large end, as the knot needs to pass back and forth.

Amazing FACTS

Knots make a rope weaker: most reduce its strength by a third. The ropes cavers use are very strong to account for this reduction in strength.

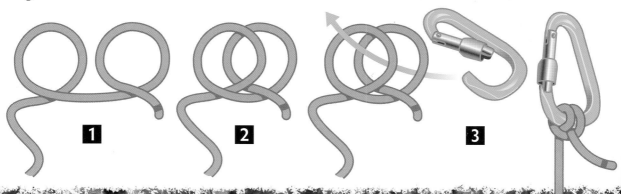

1 **2** **3**

Going Underground

Once you've joined a club and have the right clothes and equipment, you are ready to visit your first cave. You are about to experience the thrill of adventure and the wonder and beauty of these underground places.

Access to the Cave

Get an accurate weather forecast and go with experienced cavers who have been there before. There are guidebooks to many cave systems around the world that describe system sections and give you an idea what to expect.

TRUE Survivors

In August 2011, a group of eight cavers between ages 16 and 20 set off to explore a well-known North Yorkshire cavern. But shortly after they entered the caving system, water levels inside began to rise as a result of heavy rain over the previous few days. Eventually the group found themselves trapped in Lower Long Churn Cave.

Another team of cavers had spotted the group entering the caves and alerted the emergency services. A team of 26 volunteers from the Cave Rescue Organization (CRO) began a rescue operation. Five hours after the group had become trapped, they were led to safety—just minutes before the waters rose farther. They were cold and wet but uninjured after their ordeal. Dave Gallivan of the CRO said:

"If we had not got the group out at that moment, we could have all been trapped inside. It was a very lucky escape for everyone ... It was a massive error of judgment to go into this cave system considering the weather."

Long Churn Caves

Cave Grades

The cave grading system tells you in advance how difficult a cave is to explore. There are five levels of difficulty.

Grade 1 An easy cave that requires no equipment other than a helmet and a flashlight. Route finding is easy and you can walk through the passages. Suitable for beginners and children.

Grade 2 Also an easy cave that you can visit wearing just a helmet and headlamp. There might be sections that you have to squeeze through or climb over. Suitable for beginners.

Grade 3 You need to know about caving technique or be with experienced cavers when visiting grade 3 caves. Sections will be difficult and route finding could be tricky.

Grade 4 Caves at this level have hazards such as big drops, underground water, and route finding problems. You need special equipment—ropes, harnesses, abseil devices, and emergency gear—as well as helmet and headlamp.

Grade 5 The hardest level. You should have lots of experience before venturing in. The hazards and route finding will be very difficult. You need special equipment, a guidebook, and a guide to help you get in and out safely.

Squeezes and Siphons

There are special terms for the features you come across in caves. It's useful to know some of the more common ones.

Squeezes and Siphons

A squeeze is a really tight part of a passage that you have to crawl and wriggle through. Squeezes can be scary and you'll need a guide for your first few. A siphon is a U-shaped part of a passage that is filled with water. Siphons are very dangerous and should not be attempted unless you have a lot of experience and are with people who have been through them before.

You need good climbing skills when you go into a difficult cave like this.

Chambers and Passages

A chamber is a large open space in a big cave system. A confined passage might suddenly open out into a large echoing area. A passage is like a tunnel—longer than it is wide. It often connects other features, such as chambers.

Chimneys and Chokes

A chimney is a tight vertical opening in the rock. Cavers climb up a chimney in two ways. The first is to put their back on one wall and feet on the other and push their way up. Or they put one foot on one wall and the other foot on the opposite wall and push with hands and feet to ascend. A choke is a passage that is blocked, often because of a rock fall, which is one of the many hazards you meet underground.

TRUE Survivors

Someone has to be the first to explore a new cave. These explorers risk their lives, as they do not know what is around the next corner. If they have to dive through flooded passages, the danger is greater. In 1967, Steve Barnett and Dave Jagnow found Coldwater Cave in Iowa. Barnett explored the first section on his own, diving into water that was just 48°F (9°C). Over a series of explorations, the two men gradually ventured farther and farther into the cave system. On their fifth journey, they spent 52 hours surveying, and traveled almost 4 miles (6 km) underground. Today, there are 7 miles (11 km) of known passages in this system and there may be still more to explore.

Amazing Rock Formations

There are also terms for the extraordinary rock features that cavers see underground. These are often formed by the action of water and rock minerals.

Magical Minerals

Cave pearls form in hollows in a cave floor in pools of water that have minerals in them. They are made when grains of sand become coated in the mineral deposits.

These cave pearls are made from the minerals in underground water.

Helictites are delicate and beautiful fronds of mineral deposits that seem to grow out of the rock like flowers. They are not often seen in frequently visited caves as they are very fragile and can be broken by the gentlest touch.

Stalagmites and Stalactites

These form where water that has minerals in it drips through the ceiling of a chamber. The formations that grow up from the ground are called stalagmites and the ones that grow down from the ceiling are stalactites. If the two meet, they form a column.

Flowstone

Flowstone is also created by water that carries lots of minerals. Instead of dripping off a ceiling, the water flows over rock, coating it and then hardening to form a beautiful new layer. The formation can look like a frozen waterfall.

AMACING CAVES

There is a cave in Mexico known as the Cave of the Crystals. Here you can see some of the largest natural crystals on earth. Some have grown to be 36 feet (11 m) long!

TRUE Survivors

Some caves are not made of rock or deep underground. In 1982, Phil Doole and Mark Inglis were climbing on Aoraki Mount Cook, New Zealand's highest mountain, when they were caught in a storm and blizzard conditions. They crawled into an ice cave, where they were forced to stay for almost two weeks because of the extreme weather. The men had little food and were lucky to survive. When rescuers finally reached them, they had such severely frostbitten legs that both had to have their legs amputated. But this did not deter them, and in 2002, Mark Inglis became the first double amputee to reach the summit of Mount Everest.

Extreme Caving

Like all sports, caving is taken to the extreme by some people. They become very good at the sport and want to push the boundaries farther.

There is a cave in Mexico called the Cave of the Swallows. It is a large opening in the ground that goes straight down for 1,093 feet (333 m). You could stand several skyscrapers on top of each other inside it and it would take 12 seconds to hit the bottom if you jumped. Some crazy cavers make a special trip to this cave, strap on a parachute, and jump off the edge. They have very little time for the parachute to open and stop them from killing themselves. Talk about an extreme way to explore a cave!

Exploration

This is the purest form of extreme caving and also how the sport started in nineteenth century Europe and early twentieth century America. Someone has to be the first to go into a cave system and see where it leads, but with no guide or map, they have to go carefully.

Cave Digging

Cave digging is part of exploring and opening up new passageways. People use tools and sometimes even explosives to clear a way through to new areas. It can be very dangerous as there are often rock falls.

Cave Diving

Cave diving is a dangerous pastime because the risk of drowning is high. Divers need to be able to use diving equipment. A cave diver in trouble can't just swim to the surface as they would in the sea because they are surrounded by rock as well as water. There can be strong currents in underground rivers, which can trap a diver against the rock. Visibility is another problem. Cave divers take three sets of lights in case one fails.

Left A cave diver explores a stunning underwater cavern on an island in Palau in the Pacific Ocean.

TRUE Survivors

In 1988, a team of cave divers led by Andrew Wright were exploring new underwater cave systems in the Nullarbor Plains in Australia. Then a storm on the surface caved in the entrance and trapped them inside. There were parts of the cave where they could escape the water, otherwise they would all have eventually run out of air and died. Amazingly, they found another way out, but it took them almost two days to do so.

Caving Around the World

There are amazing caves of varying levels of difficulty all over the world.

The United States

Mammoth Cave in Kentucky is one of the most famous in the world. There are also caves in Tennessee, Alabama, Texas, and South Dakota. New Mexico is home to the Carlsbad Caverns and the Lechuguilla Cave.

Europe

Some of the best caves in the UK are in Yorkshire (Gaping Ghyll and Alum Pot) and South Wales (Dan yr Ogof and Ogof Fynnon Ddu). France has the very deep Réseau Jean and Gouffre Mirolda, and Spain has the Torca del Cerro and Sistema del Trave. Italy, Switzerland, and Slovenia also have big cave systems.

Alum Pot Cave, UK

Mexico

Mexico is a popular destination for avid cavers. The east has high limestone mountains and lots of rainfall, which contribute to cave formation. Famous caves include the Cave of the Swallows and the Cave of the Crystals.

New Zealand and Australia

The South Island of New Zealand has some great caving destinations in fantastic surroundings. Nettlebed Cave in Mount Arthur is 15 miles (24 km) long. On North Island, you can find the famous and unique Waitomo

Nettlebed Cave, NZ

Glowworm cave, where insects spin nests of silk and hang down from the ceiling like little stars shining in the night. The Australian island Tasmania has some popular caves, including the show cave called Gunns Plains Cave.

Africa

From the Wit Tamdoun cave in Morocco in the north, to Namibia in the south, Africa has plenty to attract cavers. South Africa has the amazing Wonder Cave that may be more than two billion years old. Its chamber is a vast 82 feet (25 m) long, 505 feet (154 m) wide, and 197 feet (60 m) deep.

Asia

China has huge caves, including the Gebihe Cave, which has one large chamber called the Miao Room. There is even a school inside a cave called the Donghzong Cave. The Islands of Malaysia and Indonesia also have huge caves. Deer Cave on Borneo has the largest passage of any cave in the world, which is an average of 230 feet (70 m) wide.

Deer Cave, Borneo

What do you know about caving?

Do you think you're ready to take on the challenge of going deep underground into wild caves? Would you know a stalagmite from a stalactite? Take this quiz to find out just how much you do know about the great underground world. The answers are on page 31.

1 Which of these statements is correct?
a You never find caves on the coast.
b Caves are natural formations found in rock all around the world.
c Limestone is the most common type of rock you find in caves.
d You don't need to wear a helmet in a cave.
e There are many caving clubs you can join.

2 Which of these is not a hazard you would find in a cave?
a Darkness
b Flowing water
c Rock fall
d Dazzling sunlight

3 Which of these is the deepest known cave in the world?
a Mammoth Cave, Kentucky
b Krubera-Voronja Cave, Georgia
c The Cave of the Crystals, Mexico
d Gaping Ghyll, Britain

4 You have to pay to get into most show caves and they are suitable for children and beginners. True or false?

5 **Why should you always take a spare flashlight into a cave?**

a In case you want to shine one in front of you and one behind

b To illuminate all the wonderful rock formations

c As part of your emergency kit, just in case your main flashlight fails

d In case you meet someone who has forgotten theirs

6 **What is a squeeze?**

a A special hug you give your team when you come out of a cave

b A term cavers use for the trucks they carry their gear in

c The special rock formations that hang down from the ceiling

d A very tight passage you have to wriggle through, often on your belly

7 **A stalactite grows up from the floor of a cave.** True or false?

8 **The cave grading system goes from 1 to 5, with 5 being the easiest type of cave.** True or false?

9 **Which of these items are not essential when you go caving?**

a Warm clothing **b** A headlamp **c** Sunscreen **d** A map
e A portable gaming system **f** Good footwear **g** A swimsuit

▼ **10** **Name these cavers' knots**

1

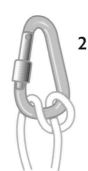

2

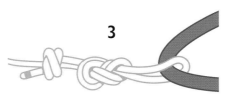

3

4

Glossary

abseil To slide down a rope using a harness and special device that allows you to control your speed and stop.

anchor A secure place you can attach yourself to using the rope tied to your harness or a sling.

base layer The layer of clothing next to the skin.

bight A small section of rope doubled over to form a loop.

carabiner A metal ring that has a gate in it that can be opened and shut to fasten a rope to it.

deposited Laid down by water; fine grains of rock deposited on the seabed or in a cave will form a thick layer over millions of years.

extinct A species of plant or animal that no longer exists on earth.

glacier A river of ice that forms over thousands of years; glaciers flow down valleys, gouging out the landscape as they do so.

halogen A group of elements, including iodine, bromine, chlorine, and fluorine; in gas form, they help to produce a very good light for using in flashlights.

hypothermia When the body's core temperature drops dangerously low and someone may become unconscious and eventually die.

lava Molten rock that flows out of a volcano.

LED Light-emitting diode, often used in making headlamps; LEDs use very little battery energy, so they last a long time.

limestone A type of rock made over millions of years from the bones of tiny sea creatures lying on the seabed; over time, this layer builds up to form a rocky bed.

national park An area of land the government sets aside where people can enjoy the natural environment; national parks are often in mountain regions, on coasts, and around rivers and wetlands.

Neanderthals An extinct species of early human that lived in ice-age Europe from about 120,000 to about 35,000 years ago.

neoprene A special type of rubber that is waterproof and warm.

pioneer Someone who goes first; the first person to explore a new cave is a pioneer.

prehistoric Something that happened or existed before history was written down.

species A type or kind of an animal or a plant.

thermals Clothing worn to help us keep warm; wool and artificial fibers both have thermal properties and are worn underneath other layers of clothing to keep people warm.

Websites

www.caves.org The US National Speleological Society

www.british-caving.org.uk The British Caving Association

www.caves.org.au The Australian Speleological Federation

www.caves.org.nz The New Zealand Speleological Society

Books

Caving Adventures (Dangerous Adventures)
  Anne M. Todd, Capstone High-Interest Books, 2002
Caving (Radical Sports) Chris Howes, Heinemann Library,
  2003
Caving (Torque: Action Sports) Jack David, Bellwether, 2009
Exploring Caves (Geography Zone) Melody S. Mis, PowerKids Press, 2009

Quiz Answers

1 *b, c, and e*

2 *d*

3 *b*

4 *True*

5 *c*

6 *d*

7 *False*

8 *False*

9 *c, e, and g*

10
  a Clove hitch
  b Italian hitch
  c Rethreaded figure-eight
  d Figure-eight on the bight

Index

abseiling 8, 10, 12, 13, 19
anchors 16, 17
archaeologists 5

carabiners 17
cave diving 21, 25
cave paintings 5
cave pearls 22
chambers 6, 8, 14, 21, 23, 27
chimneys 21
chokes 21
cliffs 6, 8
clothing 11, 14, 15, 18
clubs 10, 18
coasts 6
crystals 23, 26

deepest caves 9, 11

emergency equipment 15, 19

first aid 15
flooding 5, 14, 21
flowstone 8, 23
food 14, 15

geologists 5
glaciers 6

grades 19
guidebooks 18, 19

harnesses 12, 13, 16, 17, 19
headlamps 12, 14, 15, 19
helictites 22
helmets 12, 19
hypothermia 14

knots 16–17

ladders 7, 12
lakes 8
landslides 5
lava 6
lighting 7, 12, 25
limestone 6, 8, 26

maps 14, 25
Martel, Edouard-Alfred 5
minerals 22, 23

passages 8, 11, 14, 15, 19, 20, 21, 27
pocket knife 15

rain 6, 14, 18, 26
rivers 6, 8, 11, 15, 25
rock falls 21, 25

ropes 5, 7, 10, 12, 13, 14, 16, 17, 19

safety 7, 10, 11, 14–15, 18
show caves 7, 27
siphons 20
squeezes 20
stalactites 8, 23
stalagmites 8, 23
survival bags 15

tools 7, 25
tunnels 6, 8, 14, 21

water 14, 15
weather forecasts 14, 18